J.

And Other Poems Do

By

Joseph Chastain

Dedicated to much Love to Several women in my life:

Jennifer Deves, Anna M. Garcia, Kristin Nicole Molina, Tiffany Whitten, The memories of Dorothy Whitten Shannon Kincaid, and Sandra A. Hernandez

A few Men:

Michael Bruce Williams JR, Gordon Cornell Layne, Eric W. Chastain, Ric Rivas, Gilbert Archuletta, my Father Richard Charles Chastain

But most of all to the memory of my Mother

Ruth Ann Chastain.

And yes this is the longest dedication in history.

Mourning Star:

A poem of Justice.

I am the most hated angel

I am the most loved demon

I am the star of the morning

I am the sun of the night

My face is the face of the millions

My voice is the voice of the voiceless

My name is one that cannot be said

I walk in the burning desert

I swim in the deepest ocean

Me? I am the law of the land

I am the head of the body

You? You are the one I have found

You are perfect...but you need a little work.

I am justice, and I am not dead.

You will find me, when you stop looking.

Secrets:

A Poem of Love

Chromatic and invisible, isolated and grouped

It is freeing and confining, all things to all people

When we are one, when we are whole, it is there

There is nothing but our two bodies intertwined

There is nothing but our voices heard in the dark

There is nothing but our souls connected in place

There is nothing but our eyes looking at each other

Why do we seek to become nothing and everything

Because destinies have brought us here.

Tonight we weigh less than a feather in the wind

Tonight we see God staring at us as we stare at him

Tonight we are the same. Tonight we are one.

Two minds, two hearts, two bodies. Fear does not exist

There is no pain, there is no grief, there is no rage.

Tell me what you know, take me to your secret place.

Behold what we seek. Behold what secrets we unlock.

Requiem

A poem of Grief

Dedicated to Sandra A. Hernandez

Requiem for a love

Love unrequited

Love unresolved.

I would give up

The light of dawn

To see your face

The sound of music

To listen to your voice

And my very life

To hear "I love you"

again.

The Day After:

A poem of Bereavement

Dedicated to my mother.

It feels like life should stop moving

But it doesn't life still goes on

It feels like the world should be weeping

But only a few seem to care

It feels like I will weep forever

But I know someday I will breathe again

Maybe it's not goodbye, maybe it's see you soon

But I know until that day

Every Part of me aches, for every part of you.

Johari Window

A poem of loneliness

Darkness engulfs me like an eclipse in my mind,
I miss your smile and joy you left behind
I can't be anything more than what i am now
if I could change i wish that i knew how
although I may be as ugly as midnight's sin
open now Johari window and learn to let me in

as I mourn at the grave that was once called we
I wonder will you ever weep for me
and when we last said our loneliest goodbyes
can we end the hurt, the blame the lies
will we ever be able to be where we were again
learn to open Johari window and let me in.

so in the end i pray that will can please rebegin
to go back to what we were way back then
once last chance to see the light in your eyes
that i will worship until it is that all hope dies
is it too late for the healing to begin?
learn to open Johari window and let me in

and when you open it open it loud

and when you speak it speak it proud

know the word that i will forever speak

when the meaning i still always seek

may we open then at the final close

and the ending be the thing that shows

darkness engulfs me like an eclipse in my mind,

I miss your smile and joy you left behind

I can't be anything more than what i am now

if I could change i wish that i knew how

although I may be as ugly as midnight's sin

open now Johari window and learn to let me in

Fade to Black, cut the reels

A Poem of frustration

Think you clever trying to mate Isis with Dionysus

Giving up all for all the world to see to make capital

Make the world a better place for your stockbrokers

Fade to black, cut the reel. Light the set

God's art has become a game, fade to black cute the reel

You make a buck and that's all that counts, all you know

All the kings horses and all the kings me can't do again

Spit on the graves of those who went before, break wills

Fade to black, cut the reel, who cares if anyone feels?

Sinner's Bible:

A poem of longing.

My life is a Sinner's Bible. The verses and chapters are words
I cannot read.

The hero is not a prophet but a madman that I have set to bleed.

He searches the day for a love-- A love that he will find in
the night.

Please God let him find one person to protect him. And lead
him to the light.

To Love

A poem of desire

To love

To turn hell into Heaven

To cross bridges

To know the answers to our questions

To speak

To sigh

To answer

To raise you hands to the sky

To run to the right direction

To know contentment

To cry

To weep

To die

To love.

Walk

A poem of Hope

If I can walk

I will rule the world

If I can walk

I will be the king

If I can walk

I will one day fly

If I can walk

I will never die

Find the days

When I wasn't whole

Make the most

Of each passing hour

Hold my head up high

And no longer know pain

If I should walk

I would be content

If I should walk

I would be reborn

If I should walk

I would be pure

If I should walk

I would be myself

And I will speak to God

Find my world again

And all shall speak my name

For I shall be the first

To ever find a new life.

Song of Songs

A poem of Childhood.

When I was a child my mother sang to me

the song of songs that made me feel so free

I swore on everything I'd write another song

that would make all men stand up strong

mother where are you now sing to me again

I pray someday I'll hold you in my arms then

song of songs that fills me with wonder

feel the pain and joy that i am under

fill my heart with feelings from god above

let me know what it means to feel love

when i was a boy my grandma said i can

be just as special as any other man

to show her i remember her i have made a vow

o remember them I'll write a song

unless I can share love they've shown

when was a child my mother sang to me

the song of songs that made me feel so free

now she's dead I must right those wrongs

so I'll write for her the song of songs

By any other Name

A poem of Envy

by any other name would i smell as sweet?

if I were someone else would i be your treat

I wish i was the same to you as he

but I finally know it isn't meant to be

please don't hate me
please let me be
please don't hate me
please let me be
by any other name, could you show me love
if I were him could I be your dove?
please don't hate me
please let me be
please don't hate me
please let me be
by any other name would I not be hurt
by any other name would I be like dirt?
by any other name would you hold me?
by any other name would you set me free?
please don't hate me
please let me be
please don't hate me
please let me be
by any other name would I smell as sweet?

if I were someone else would i be your treat

I wish i was the same to you as he

but I finally know it isn't meant to be

Untitled

A poem of pain.

Falling

Flying

Finding

Nothing

Seeing

Hearing

Feeling

Nothing

Love

Gone

Hurt

Feeling

Hearing

Seeing

Everything

What

Can

I

Do

To

End

This

Heartache

Help

Me

This Is for You

A poem of inspiration

Read this closely

Inside this poem is the answer

I wrote it for you

Yes you and only you

You know who you are...

You're the one reading it.

You are special

You are worthy

Read this closely

This poem is for you

God wanted me to tell you

You will be okay today

And every other day

God told me that

Not the God that you read about as a child

That lives on a fluffy white cloud.

But God, who lives inside humans

He wanted to say, he loves you.

And he wanted me to write this poem for you,

And only you,

And no one else.

Just you.

I hope that made you feel special.

This poem is for everyone.

And just you.

Gods Tears

A poem of passion

Your beauty made God cry

Your love made the angels sigh

Your voice made heaven rain

Your heart made creation pain

For you are enough to take away my fears

But you are enough to create gods tears

When you were born life began again

And the world went to where it had been

Inside your eyes is love

Enough for the lord above

Inside your smile is joy

That no darkness can destroy

The planet opens at your breath

Your absence is the pangs of death

Your voice is what my heart hears

And without is even God shed's tears.

I'm Still Alive

A poem of determination

Chromatic invisibility fills my eyes,

silence screams inside my ears,

beauty and pain are equal,

I raise my hands,

Kill me once

Kill me twice

Kill me until I live

Take all that I am

I'm still alive

Rob me, rape me, throw me into a pit.

Break me, burn me, bite me, bound me

Murder me make me scream

I am deaf though I hear

I am blind but I see...

I'm still alive.

Tell me I have no hope,

throw me into the cages,

whip me until I bleed

stone me until I bruise,

Imprison me, incarcerate me

Take my family, take my friends,

I'm still alive.

Rip out my eyes,

Pierce my tongue,

Stab my chest,

Cut off my hands,

Flog my back,

I'm still alive.

Through the Horrors,

Through the betrayals,

Through the torture,

Through the loss,

Through the setbacks,

I'M STILL ALIVE

YOU'RE STILL ALIVE

WE'RE STILL ALIVE.

SAY IT OUTLOUD

SCREAM IT FROM THE ROOFTOPS

I'M STILL ALIVE

And until our last breath happens

Until the last words spoken

Until our final thought goes through our head

Until the end of all our journeys

We will still stand

We will not give in/

I'M STILL ALIVE

YOU'RE STILL ALIVE

WE'RE STILL ALIVE.

SAY IT OUTLOUD

Pronounce it to the stars

I'M STILL ALIVE

We will hold onto this for our lives.

We will not give in.

We will stand up for what is right,

We will protect the weak

We will help the poor.

I'M STILL ALIVE

YOU'RE STILL ALIVE

WE'RE STILL ALIVE.

SAY IT OUTLOUD

Yell it to the moon

I'M STILL ALIVE

Why

A poem of hope

Why is my life shattered?

Why is my mind in shadow?

Why do I not see the path once clear?

Why do I feel like the end is near?

Hold me, feel me, touch me, see me, know who I am.

I will find my way and it will be dawn again.

For darkness cannot exist at the same time as light

Pain cannot exist at the same time as health

Hate cannot exist at the same time as love

And cold cannot exist at the same time as warmth

Why if I am damaged do I still fight?

Why if I am alone do I still seek joy?

Why is do I keep going when all stop?

Why do I feel my heart beat when I ache?

Hold me, feel me, touch me, see me, know who I am.

I will find my way and it will be dawn again.

Suddenly

A poem of adoration

Suddenly I see the love inside of me.

Suddenly I hear a voice free from fear.

Suddenly I know the love that will grow

Suddenly I feel the heart that is real.

How did I know this would be the first time?

How did I know this would be the last as well?

Suddenly the Earth opens up to swallow me

Suddenly I feel out hearts becoming one

My peace is in your eyes and in all I am

My joy is in your voice and all I will be

Suddenly you call my name and I answer

Suddenly I feel your light inside of me

Suddenly I am a man born again and anew

Suddenly I feel your hand touching me

Suddenly I see your smile in my mind

Suddenly I feel the joy I thought died

Misread Angel

A poem of Comfort

See the truth in my eyes

 as your fear slowly dies

when you let go of your tears

the misread angel appears he knows the words you long to hear

and the things you hold dear

he longs to show you brighter days

or will you misread his ways?

this misread angel, where does he dwell

halfway to heaven and halfway to hell

he longs to take you into the light

this misread angel of night

See the pain on his face

 and the light of his grace

darkness will never win

 as long as you do not give in

this misread angel how has he fell

it's been so long no one can tell

he longs to take you into the light

this misread angel of night

this misread angel where is he now

he'll make you happy he doesn't care how

he longs to take you into the light

this misread angel of night

There was a light

A poem of righteousness

From his first breath I was watching him

in a world that at first seemed so dim

from every truth and every lie

every how every what and every why

I saw his every sight heard all he heard

thought his thoughts spoke his words

his birth was not marked by a star

no wise men came to him from afar

no shepherds were apart from their round

he was not in a manger's crib found was

he was not a messiah or even a prophet found

still there was a light that shined

so bright it left most of us blind

there was a light there was a light

it was a beacon in the cold night

I saw everything he saw and I saw there was a light...

He Loves Us...

A poem of faith

No matter if we are a king or crook

Even if we've never read a book

No matter what sin's we've done

To him we are his daughter or son

He loves us so much.

Each moment we breathe it is the same

Each moment is a blessing in his name

Each moment is one to cherish

Each moment that we don't perish

He loves us so much

If there ever is a moment

When doubt is my opponent

I just remember this poem

And it will guide me home

He loves us so much

Song Of Songs...

A Poem of memories.

When I was a child My mother sang to me

The song of songs that made me feel so free

I swore then I'd write another song

That would make all men stand up so strong

Mother where are you to sing to me again?

I pray someday you'll hold me in your arms then

Sing the song of songs with endless wonder

And you will feel the joy and pain I am under

When I was a child my grandma said I can

Be just as great as any other man

They're both gone I know this now

So to them I've made this solemn vow

They will never ever be known

Unless I can show the love they shown

When I was a child my mother sang to me

The song of songs that made me feel so free

Now she is dead and I must right these wrongs

By giving all of you the song of songs...

JOSEPH CHASTAIN

Has been writing poetry since he was a small child.

He has had a few poems published and has written Newspaper and Magazine articles.

He has a B.A. in film and Television from Columbia College Hollywood and also attended San Bernardino Valley College where he studied anything they'd legally let him.

He lives in San Bernardino, California, where he often writes screenplays, novels or short stories in addition to poetry and he works on the occasional film.

Made in the USA
Las Vegas, NV
02 March 2022

44913344R00022